1 Introduction

A large and growing literature demonstrates theoretically and empirically that firms offering multiple differentiated products in the same market incur both costs and benefits.[1] Economists also have long devoted attention to showing how agency theory (Holmstrom and Milgrom, 1991), transactions costs (Williamson, 1975), and the property rights theory of the firm (Grossman and Hart, 1986, Hart and Moore, 1990) may explain firm boundaries, finding much support for their predictions across a variety of contexts (Lafontaine and Slade, 2007). Considering the richness of these literatures, comparatively little attention has gone to understanding how they may intersect. In particular, there is little treatment of the interrelated questions of how market structure could influence the choice of vertical contracts and how vertical contracts could lead to different product market behavior depending on the local market structure.

I address these gaps by investigating the relationship between market structure and vertical contracting in the retail gasoline industry. It is an ideal setting to consider these issues as a gasoline refiner may have multiple stations in a given market selling their gasoline. (I refer to stations sharing the same refiner brand as being "affiliated.") Moreover, refiners' affiliated stations may be operated under two different classes of contract. The first type is vertically integrated insofar as refiner employees staff the station, and the refiner remains the residual claimant. In contrast, the second class of contract makes local managers the residual claimants and allocates them extensive control rights. It is thus an example of vertical separation.

The principal-agent framework straightforwardly extends to suggest why a vertically separated station should behave differently than an integrated one in markets where there is (are) one (or more) affiliated station(s). By virtue of being the residual claimant, managers at vertically separated stations are incentivized to prioritize the performance of their station. Therefore, when choosing their profit-maximizing strategies, a vertically separated station manager will only pay attention to

---

[1] A benefit might be deterring entry by competitors, while the costs could include cannibalizing revenue from their existing products. See discussion in Sutton (2007).

the impact of a strategy's impact on their station's profits. They ignore any impact of those strategies on affiliated stations. In contrast, the manager of a vertically integrated station's incentives are not so narrowly focused, and their strategy may incorporate the effects on all affiliated stations.

Left unrestrained, the tendency of vertically separated stations to ignore the competitive externalities of their product market behavior on affiliated stations would cause the joint profits of all affiliated stations in the market to be lower than the profit-maximizing level. Therefore, the existence of affiliated stations in a given market increases refiners' exposure to moral hazard if they use a vertically separated contract. Thus, market structure can be thought of in the same light as other forms of moral hazard caused by vertical separation (Klein, 1980, 1995, Brickley and Dark, 1987, Brickley, 1999, Laffont and Martimort, 2002).

As noted in Winter (2009), the legal system makes it difficult for principals like refiners to contractually restrain pro-competitive behavior (like price-cutting) on the part of their agents. Therefore, economic behavior on the part of both vertically-separated station managers and refiners should vary depending on local market structure. Exploiting rich data on retail gasoline markets, I test this prediction. My chief findings regarding the empirical importance of competition-driven moral hazard are as follows.

First, the data show that gasoline refiners are more likely to employ vertically separated contracts in markets where they have fewer affiliated stations. This result is consistent with a desire to avoid the type of competition-driven moral hazard described above. However, I find evidence of monitoring complementarities from the presence of other vertically separated outlets. Specifically, the data show that the greater the share of nearby affiliated outlets operated under vertically separated contracts, the greater the likelihood that another outlet will be vertically separated. This result suggests that the marginal cost of monitoring an additional station is lower in areas where monitoring must already take place, an idea exploited in several recent papers considering the impact of organizational form on economic behavior (Kosova et al., 2010, Wilson, 2011b).

Second, using a difference in differences approach to estimation, I find that the presence of affiliated stations is correlated with different economic behaviors depending on whether a station is operated under a vertically separated or vertically integrated contract. For example, stations operated under vertically separated contracts are more likely to reduce prices as the affiliated presence increases. This effect is consistent with the idea that sharing a local market produces moral hazard for managers at vertically separated stations who are not incentivized to price "cooperatively." Moreover, I show that the quality of vertically separated stations' appearances are decreasing in the number of affiliated outlets in the market. This result is in line with the idea that consumers are influenced by the local reputation of a given brand in making their purchasing decisions. Thus, there is an externality to quality provision much as there is for "cooperative" pricing.

Overall, the paper contributes to a number of literatures. First, it extends the small but growing body of work assessing how economic behavior varies across vertical contracts (Novak and Stern, 2008, Forbes and Lederman, 2010, Kosova et al., 2010, Wilson, 2011b). These papers have expanded on much of the previous vertical contracting literature by more explicitly accounting for the endogeneity of contracts. However, they concentrate on characteristics that might be thought to affect the choice, and subsequent behavior, for traditional agency theoretic and/or transactions costs reasons, abstracting from the competition-related factors focused upon in this paper. Like previous papers within this literature focusing on the gasoline industry (Barron and Umbeck, 1984, Vita, 2000, Wilson, 2011b), I find that vertical separation is correlated with higher prices. The present work extends the prior literature by showing that the magnitude of the vertical separation effect is correlated with a function of local market structure.

Second, the paper contributes to a line of research focusing on intra-firm competition in franchise industries. Hadfield (1991) points out that vertically separating control of multiple outlets may successfully enable an incumbent franchisor to deter entry from competing firms. However, in practice, agents are thought to fear that any potential benefits from softer intra-brand competition will be swamped by the cannibalization effect of customer stealing by affiliated outlets. Kalnins (2004) and Wilson (2011a) present evidence that such fears of "encroachment" are justified in hotel markets, while Thomadsen (2005) documents intensified competition between affiliated fast food outlets. The present paper contributes to this literature by documenting behavioral variation depending on the local market structure in the gasoline industry. Moreover, my results on quality determination are consistent with the idea that encroachment matters not just in terms of revenue cannibalization, but also in its implications for reputational free-riding.

The paper proceeds as follows. In section 2, I sketch the theoretical intuition for expecting behavior at vertically separated stations to differ in multi-product markets. Section 3 describes the institutional characteristics of the retail gasoline industry, while section 4 discusses the data used to test the hypotheses highlighted in section 2. Sections 5 and 6 present econometric analyses of how contract utilization and behavior vary with local market structure. The paper concludes in section 6.

2 Market Structure and Vertical Separation

Agency problems arise when employers cannot perfectly infer employee effort from observable information. Franchise and other vertically separated contracts address this problem by tying local agents' (i.e., franchisees) salaries to some visually observable performance metric. This helps to better align their incentives with those of the principal (i.e., franchisor). When two contracts have the same expected value for agent compensation, the contract with the higher variable component is considered "higher-powered." This is because it gives stronger incentives (i.e., higher residual claims) to the local agent to exert costly effort.[2]

While vertically separated contracts tie compensation to local performance in order to elicit higher effort, they also frequently contain provisions constraining elements of agent behavior. This is because principals' interests are rarely one dimensional. In addition to wanting to maximize static

---

[2]Agents' ownership of the local assets is not a prerequisite for a vertically separated contract; rather, it is such contracts' transfer of the right to residual claims and the ability of agents to influence them that are critical elements to focus upon. In practice, most vertically-separated contracts turn over control rights to the local agent, while the principal receives a portion of the outlet's total revenues in return for allowing agents the right to affiliate with their brand. The remainder of the local revenues are kept by the agent. Depending on the industry, agents' ownership of the local assets varies.

profits, principals frequently have dynamic concerns related to things like brand equity, which they may fear that local managers will not value. For example, Brickley and Dark (1987) note that when customers are unlikely to visit a given outlet again, an agent with a high-powered contract may shirk on those elements that go to maintaining the brand's reputation. Brickley and Dark (1987) argued that this suggests that vertically separated contracts should be less likely to be used in environments where the likelihood of non-repeat customers was high.[3]

Because of such concerns, the overall viability of vertically separated contracts depends crucially on the ability of the principal to observe and punish agents' deviations from specified behavior. Consistent with this, Brickley et al. (1991) show that vertically separated contracts are less likely to be used in U.S. states that have laws inhibiting the termination of franchise contracts.

It is straightforward to see why moral hazard problems similar to those noted by Brickley and Dark (1987) may arise if there are multiple affiliated outlets in the same market. Consider the example of a retail industry where branded outlets compete on factors influenced by the local manager's efforts. The brand-owner is the contract-offering principal, while the manager of a local outlet is the agent. The brand-owner can employ either low-powered contracts, which involve using salaried employees to manage an outlet, or high-powered vertically separated contracts that give the local manager a direct stake as well as control over the locally determined factors influencing sales.

Assume that the market is sufficiently large for the brand-owner to choose to open two outlets. Because the principal's benefit derives from the performance of both outlets, it would prefer that they adopt strategies maximizing their joint profits. This is what will occur if the principal uses its own salaried employees at both stations. If, however, the principal uses different high-powered agents, it could lead to either more or less intense competition than the principal would prefer.[4]

For example, if competition takes place in prices, then the high-powered agents will price lower

---

[3]This prediction was born out in the authors' cross-industry analyses. However, tests just using data on fast food outlets were less obviously supportive.

[4]The story applies equally to settings where one outlet is vertically integrated and one is vertically separated. The crucial detail is that ownership is not unified.

than the principal would prefer to try to steal sales from the other outlet. Thus, agents are excessively competing from the perspective of the principal. By contrast, if demand is influenced by a brand's local reputation for quality, high-powered agents will be more inclined to free-ride since they do not reap the full benefit of investments in a brand's reputation.[5] In this case, the agents are choosing a less intense strategy than the principal would prefer. For both situations, the problem is that the high-powered agent does not internalize the competition-related externality from their actions.

This competition-driven moral hazard would be very difficult for the principal to inhibit once contracts had been chosen. While prices might seem easy to observe, there remains considerable ambiguity about the legality of disciplining an agent for doing pro-competitive things like reducing prices (Winter, 2009). As a result, franchise contracts typically do not permit a principal to mandate price floors (Blair and Lafontaine, 2005). There are no such questions about the legitimacy of punishing agents who shirk on quality. However, identifying violators would be problematic, and navigating the court system can be difficult even in the best of circumstances (see, e.g., the anecdotes in Lafontaine et al. (2011)). Because of these types of concerns, a rational, profit-seeking principal should therefore be less likely to employ vertically separated forms in markets with (more) affiliated outlets all else equal.

It is worth noting, however, that there could be other reasons to expect local market structure to influence economic behavior and vertical contract utilization. Moreover, these other factors may undercut, or even offset, the effects of competition-driven moral hazard. First, if a franchisor already has a large number of vertically separated outlets in a given area that it must regularly monitor, then the marginal cost of monitoring an additional vertically separated outlet could be lower than somewhere it has no other stations to monitor. Such monitoring efficiencies could increase the

---

[5]The assumption that consumers are most affected by the appearance of local outlets does not seem strong. For example, it can be justified by assuming that consumers weight their opinions of brands based on their views of affiliated outlets. Insofar as consumers are likely to see local outlets more often than those far away, their perspective on a brand as a whole is likely to be especially influenced by local factors. See, e.g., Bronnenberg et al. (2009, 2010) for evidence of enduring loyalty to local brands.

desirability of separated forms in markets with more than one affiliated outlets. There is no clear prediction about how such efficiencies would impact economic behavior.

Second, Blair and Lafontaine (2006) suggest that there may be economies of scale in advertising in franchising industries. If franchisees are thought to be better at advertising and other local promotions, as they are in the retail gasoline industry (Kleit, 2005), it might also lead to greater utilization of vertically separated contracts in markets with more affiliated outlets. It should also lead to higher prices.

In many circumstances, both competition-driven moral hazard and externality-related benefits to separation may simultaneously be at work. In such circumstances, the dominant influence will be an empirical question.

3 Institutional Background

Gasoline stations can be divided into two categories. The first set of stations are those whose marquee identifies the vertically integrated refiner (e.g., Exxon or Shell) whose gas – and only whose gas – is sold there. Even though not all stations affiliated with these refiners are operated under vertically integrated contracts, they are referred to as vertically integrated. This is because they have an active branded presence in retail markets, and do not just produce gasoline for sale in the wholesale market. Kleit (2005) indicates that refiner-affiliated stations accounted for 78 percent of the industry in 2002. The remaining stations are commonly referred to as independents because as they are not tied to any particular refiner. As a result, they may purchase whatever brand of gasoline they choose in the wholesale market. Insofar as they are the dominant type of station, I focus on the issues affecting contract choice at refiner-affiliated stations.[6]

Despite the fact that gasoline stations' core product is comparatively homogeneous, gasoline

---

[6]Like the stations affiliated with vertically integrated refiners, independent stations may be branded (e.g., Sheetz). The independent brands must address many of the same agency and moral hazard issues as integrated refiners. Interestingly, preliminary regressions that included them did not lead to qualitatively different results. However, since their cost functions are different in kind from the refiner-affiliated stations, I believe it is more appropriate to exclude them. Details are available upon request.

stations engage in differentiated competition.[7] This is because retail gasoline markets vary in terms of consumer tastes and demographics. Moreover, and not unrelatedly, stations are differentiated in terms of non-gasoline "quality" (e.g., service, station cleanliness), geographic location, and the presence (or absence) of alternative services (e.g., convenience stores, repair bays).

To deal with such heterogeneity, vertically integrated gasoline refiners employ a variety of contracts that differ in their implications for local control. As has been previously recognized, these contract choices connect in a straightforward manner to principal-agent models of vertical integration and the franchising literature (see, e.g., Shepard (1993), Slade (1996)). The refiners are the principals, while individual gasoline station managers are the agents. As in other retail industries (Blair and Lafontaine, 2005), the principal (i.e., the refiner) sets the terms of the contracts, which Slade (1996) notes tend to be linear with a fixed component and a variable component connected to station sales.[8]

The first type of commonly utilized contract is one in which the station and the land on which it sits are wholly-owned by the refiners. All personnel at such "company-owned and operated" stations are salaried refiner employees, and all decision-making authority resides with the principal (i.e., the refiner). While there may be occasional intra-firm tournaments to induce extra effort from employees, the station personnel never have control over pricing, nor do they have any incentive to exert special effort to maximize local profits. As these agents' long-run career interests are tied to promotion within the firm, it is reasonable to expect them to value relatively equally profits at all affiliated stations.

In addition to this canonical example of a low-powered contract, the retail gasoline industry uses three other contracts. Each of these is a variant of traditional high-powered, vertically separated contracts wherein the principal fully transfers incentives and local control to outside parties.

---

[7]See Kleit (2005) or Hosken et al. (2008) for recent surveys of retail gasoline markets.

[8]It is rare to find a firm that uses only one type of contract. In other words, most gasoline refiners are at an "interior solution" in the words of Krueger (1991). The fact that firms commonly utilize multiple contract types has the desirable econometric implication that I can control for brand-level heterogeneity in the empirical work below; the firm-level fixed effects will not be perfectly correlated with contract choices.

However, as described further below, there are modest differences across them.[9]

The most commonly utilized of the vertically separated forms is called a "lessee dealer" arrangement. In this contract, the vertically integrated refiner still owns the land and building; however, instead of using salaried employees, the refiner leases the station to a local agent, who purchases gasoline at a price set by the refiner (see Meyer and Fischer (2004) for additional details on these arrangements). The lessee dealers then behave as entrepreneurs with respect to station operations, setting prices for gasoline and all other goods and services (including repairs if the station has service bays). Thus, local agents' incentives under lessee dealer contracts encourage them to focus only on the performance of individual stations.

The next contract closely resembles lessee dealer arrangements except that the local agent owns the land and station and, therefore, pays no rental fee to the refiner. Presumably because the local outlet is not tied through property ownership to any given refiner, the contract type is referred to as an "open dealer" arrangement.[10] Again, local managers under this contractual form are incentivized to prioritize the performance of their individual station.

The final contract type is identical to open dealer arrangements but for the fact that the owner of the land and station owns multiple stations, a situation common in other franchising industries (Kalnins and Lafontaine, 2004). These stations are often all in the same area (see, e.g., DeBonis (2011)). The owners often are branded convenience store chains or gasoline wholesalers known as "jobbers." As a result, the contract category is referred to as "jobber/wholesaler." Because of the multi-unit aspect, the final contract type is a bit different. The owner's interests span a number of units, which might be thought to attenuate focus on individual stations. In this case, the "true" local managers may be less high-powered than open dealers or lessee dealers, unless the jobber has adopted lessee dealer arrangements of its own. Regardless, however, the manager of a station operated under a jobber/wholesaler contract will not have contractual or career incentives linking

---

[9] For lengthier treatments of these different forms, see one of the many papers examining competition and form choice in this industry (Slade, 1996, Blass and Carlton, 2001, Kleit, 2005, Wilson, 2011b).

[10] Anecdotally, there is evidence bearing out the implication that open dealers can switch their affiliated refiner easily.

their station's behavior to affiliated stations unless they are owned by the same jobber/wholesaler.

Although there are important differences across the different vertically separated contracts, recent research by Wilson (2011b) suggests that lessee dealer, open dealer, and jobber stations all charge higher prices, ceteris paribus, than vertically integrated stations. I attributed this to a combination of the agents' effort-induced increases in consumer demand as well as double-marginalization. Moreover, I found that the assumption that the margin of increase in price relative to vertical integration was equal for all of these forms generally could not be rejected.[11]

In the present paper, I take advantage of this behavioral similarity to simplify the analysis, focusing on the difference between integrated (i.e., company owned and operated) and separated (i.e., lessee dealer, open dealer, and jobber) stations. (Shepard (1993) takes a similar econometric approach in her analysis of the impact of vertical separation on pricing.) To the extent that some forms – e.g., jobber-owned – may be closer to company-ownership than others, this approach will understate differences, and hence is a conservative one.[12]

4 Data

As in Wilson (2011b), I rely upon regional censuses of retail gasoline stations assembled by New Image Marketing, a consulting company, whose employees assessed observable station characteristics before talking with on-site staff about stations' ownership and other factors. In the data, stations are uniquely identified by location code within states. Restricting the sample to branded stations affiliated with refiners leaves 4687 station-period observations affiliated with 3677 different unique station location codes.[13] Although not common, some station locations do change brands during the sample period. These changes appear unrelated to changes in organizational form or other important factors.

---

[11]Wilson (2011b) presented evidence, however, that the forms may lead to different sales volumes, suggesting different proportions of effort-shifting relative to double marginalization.

[12]In Table B-3 in Appendix B, I present behavioral results when each type of contract is used. They indicate that all of the paper's baseline results are qualitatively robust to the disaggregation of contract types.

[13]The retail chains included in the branded sample are: Amoco, Ashland, BP, Chevron, Citgo, Conoco, Crown, Exxon, Marathon, Mobil, Phillips, Shamrock, Shell, Sinclair, Speedway, Super America, Sunoco, Texaco, and Total.

The operations surveyed by New Image are in the Denver, Minneapolis, Toledo, Louisville, and Washington, DC metro areas. The data are from 1996 and 1999. Table B-1 in the Appendix shows that observations are not evenly distributed across time periods or states. Moreover, Table B-2 indicates that the usage of the different forms varies widely across metro areas, which reflects – in part – the fact that some states in the sample have "divorcement" laws. These restrict refiners' ability to own and operate stations.[14] Overall, company-owned, lessee dealer, open dealer, and jobber/wholesaler contracts account for 15 percent, 39 percent, 24 percent, and 22 percent of station-year observations, respectively. The share of stations operated directly by refiners is consistent with the estimated national average of 10-20 percent cited in Kleit (2005).

In addition to considering where vertically separated contracts are employed, I analyze pricing and quality provision. In analyzing price, I use the listed prices of regular, super, and premium quality gasolines. In order to assess quality, I use New Image's impression of the appearance of the station. This variable was recorded as a categorical variable with six possible values. However, I simplify it to a binary variable taking the value of one when a station receives one of the two highest quality scores.[15]

As with much of the prior literature focusing on competition and market structure, I use zipcodes to distinguish different local markets.[16] This choice is not without its potential problems. As Mazzeo (2002) and others have noted, there can be concerns about using geographic regions to define markets, which has led some to use mileage bands (Shepard, 1993, Hosken et al., 2008). However, concerns about markets based on geographic definitions are particularly pronounced when there are large asymmetries across them.[17] Insofar as all of my zipcodes are in metropolitan areas,

---

[14] Virginia, Maryland, and the District of Columbia all have divorcement laws. As noted above, these laws limit (or prohibit) use of salaried operations. The strength of these laws varies across the different states, with those of Maryland and DC being much stronger than that of Virginia. See Vita (2000) for details on divorcement laws.

[15] The precise definition of the quality variable is given in Appendix A along with all other variables. I also record any possible transformations for use in the econometric analysis there. To ensure that the utilization of a binary choice model did not drive the results, I examined the implications of using ordered choice models under the implicit assumption of consistent grading by New Image employees. I generated qualitatively similar results.

[16] For recent examples, see Zhu et al. (2009), Berry and Waldfogel (2010), Ellickson (forthcoming).

[17] Moreover, it is worth noting that such asymmetries also may affect exogenously determined spatial definitions. See Kalnins (2004) for more discussion of this issue.

Table 1: Descriptive Statistics

Variable	Obs	Mean	Std. Dev.	Min	Max
Regular	4239	116.61	13.76	79.90	167.90
Medium	4236	126.61	13.17	86.90	186.90
Premium	4239	134.76	12.51	88.90	193.90
1(Appearance)	4612	0.15	0.36	0.00	1.00
Local Presence	4612	1.26	1.42	0.00	8.00
Share Separated	4612	0.83	0.25	0.00	1.00
Competitors	4612	9.63	6.80	0.00	36.00
1(C-Store)	4612	0.72	0.45	0.00	1.00
1(Service Bays)	4612	0.40	0.49	0.00	1.00
Nozzles	4460	18.22	9.96	2.00	60.00
Volume	4460	104.85	50.52	10.00	400.00
Pop. ('000s)	4612	620.67	295.13	40.99	1109.63
Income ('000)	4612	58.10	14.59	35.47	96.69

I believe that such problems are not likely to be acute here. Moreover, to further account for variation across markets, I obtain county-level data on population from the U.S. Census and average household income (in thousands) taken from the Statistics of Income (SOI) collected by the Internal Revenue Service to further account for market heterogeneity.[18] Finally, as I frequently have multiple observations in a given area (as well as multiple years of data for many zipcodes), I can control for unobserved geographic heterogeneity that might lead to systematic differences in behavior across areas.

To capture the character of competition facing a given station, I use the numbers of brand-affiliated and unaffiliated stations in the zipcode. The unaffiliated category includes independents as well as stations affiliated with other refiners because consumers are unlikely to discriminate between them.[19] To be specific, I model the local market structure facing a given station i, ω_i, as (A_i, N_i), where A is the number of stations sharing the same brand as the station of interest, and N is the number of all other stations. Thus, A_i is equal to one if there is one additional filling

---

[18]See http://www.census.gov/popest/counties/ and http://www.irs.gov/taxstats/article/0,,id=120303,00.html, respectively.

[19]One might reasonably be concerned that a greater share of independents indicates something about the degree of wholesale competition. Therefore, I include the fraction of local gasoline retailers accounted for by independents in robustness regressions. I did not find that it had a dramatic influence on the results.

station selling the same brand of gasoline as station i in the zipcode. Similarly, N_i would be equal to five if there were five stations affiliated either with different refiners or wholly independent of refiner networks in the zipcode.

To control for the possible existence of monitoring complementarities when assessing the desirability of using a vertically separated form, I use the share of other stations in a given county in a given year that are operated under vertically separated contracts.[20] It should be noted that this approach takes contemporaneous form choices of the affiliated outlets as predetermined, which could raise concerns about simultaneity. I do not dismiss these concerns; however, as shown below, checks exploiting the previous year's choices suggest that this approach does not lead to significantly biased results.[21] Therefore, to maximize my sample size, my baseline approach is to use the contemporaneous measure.

Besides each station's brand affiliation, the New Image data provide information on a large number of station features. These include the presence of a convenience store, the presence of service bays, and the number of fuel pump nozzles.[22] I include all these variables as controls in my analyses. I show descriptive statistics for all station-year observations in Table 1.

Table 2 shows summary statistics for all of the different outcome and explanatory variables for vertically integrated and separated stations. Consistent with Wilson (2011b), it shows that prices are consistently higher at vertically separated stations. Similarly, it shows that the "quality" (as

---

[20] I use the number of affiliated outlets in the county as opposed to the zipcode for several reasons. Primarily, this reflects the fact that I believe that conditional on traveling from their headquarters to a given county, it costs principals relatively little to travel between zipcodes to monitor different stations. In addition, because brands frequently do not have more than one outlet in a zipcode, it is hard to precisely identify the impact of contracting complementarities, though Wilson (2011b) reports that using zipcode-level shares did not qualitatively change the results of the analysis.

One might also worry that this model of monitoring costs misses important details such as differences across counties with different total numbers of stations. Therefore, I experimented with specifications that included both the number of affiliated outlets and the share (as well as an interaction term between them). This approach led to almost identical results. Therefore, I present the more parsimonious specification here. Details are available upon request.

[21] Somewhat similarly, in the models reported in the paper, I use the contemporaneous values of the number of brand-affiliated and unaffiliated stations. This might also give rise to concern about simultaneity bias. However, regressions where I replaced the contemporaneous values with one year lags led to qualitatively similar results to those presented in the paper. Given the strong degree of autocorrelation for local market structures, the tests are not dispositive. Nevertheless, I think they suggest that any simultaneity bias is of comparatively limited magnitude.

[22] In most cases, these data were collected as categorical variables. Insofar as different inspectors were utilized, I simplify the variables to dichotomous variables except in the case of relatively objective factors like the number of nozzles.

Table 2: Descriptive Statistics across Vertically Integrated and Separated Stations

		Integrated			Separated		
Variable	Obs	Mean	Std. Dev.	Obs	Mean	Std. Dev.	T-Test
Regular	657	106.63	16.37	3642	118.53	12.36	-70.74
Medium	657	117.86	14.70	3639	128.29	12.19	-65.06
Premium	657	127.03	14.11	3642	136.28	11.66	-58.88
1(Appearance)	823	0.25	0.43	3864	0.13	0.33	4.81
Local Presence	823	1.37	1.57	3864	1.22	1.38	3.08
Share Separated	823	0.47	0.36	3864	0.89	0.17	-19.13
Competitors	823	10.40	7.85	3864	9.48	6.53	8.74
1(C-Store)	823	0.67	0.47	3864	0.73	0.45	-2.34
1(Service Bays)	823	0.06	0.24	3864	0.46	0.50	-19.71
Nozzles	671	20.13	10.91	3864	17.79	9.73	17.07
Volume	671	138.63	51.25	3864	99.15	47.81	132.53
Pop. ('000s)	823	545.48	274.94	3864	634.68	295.96	-139.20
Income ('000)	823	59.21	14.55	3864	57.59	14.59	11.07

proxied for by appearance) of vertically integrated stations is consistently higher. This is in line with the findings of Michael (2000) and Jin and Leslie (2009) in other industries, and consistent with the prediction of Brickley and Dark (1987) that franchisees may not have the same incentives to exert effort on activities that benefit the entire brand.

Intuition about the strategic deployment of different contractual forms depending on local market structure can be gained by examining Table 3, which shows the breakdown of station-year observations by vertical contract type depending on the number of local affiliates. Consistent with the existence of competition-driven moral hazard, the Table indicates that a higher proportion of outlets are operated under vertically separated contracts in zipcodes without an affiliated outlet than in the sample as a whole. Moreover, there is declining utilization of vertically separated contracts as the number of affiliated outlets increases. Accordingly, the opposite results hold for vertically integrated stations. While the effects are not large, they are strikingly monotonic.

While Table 3 indicates contract usage patterns are consistent with concern about competition-driven moral hazard, one might reasonably wonder if there might be other drivers. I therefore examine if there are detectable behavioral differences across market structures and contract types

Table 3: Affiliated Presence and Contract Utilization

	Integrated	Separated	Total
Zero Affiliated	308	1,519	1,827
	16.86	*83.14*	*100*
One Affiliated	217	1,029	1,246
	17.42	*82.58*	*100*
Two Affiliated	155	703	858
	18.07	*81.93*	*100*
> Two Affiliated	143	613	756
	18.92	81.08	100
Total	823	3,864	4,687
	17.56	*82.44*	*100*

Rows in *italics* indicate percentages of observations within row.

in Table 4. The Table shows how the means of all station-year observations of prices and appearance quality vary depending on both contractual form and the number of affiliated outlets in the zipcode. The results do not indicate different trends for the prices charged by integrated and separated stations as the number of local affiliates increases. For both types of contract, there is a slight downward trend.

Table 4 shows less ambiguity, however, in the relationship between vertical separation, market structure, and the quality of stations' appearance. The Table shows a clear positive correlation between the presence of affiliated stations and the provision of quality for vertically integrated stores. This is consistent with the idea that there are positive local reputational spillovers that the principal is incentivized to internalize. By contrast, there is no trend for vertically separated outlets, which is in line with the comparative absence of any such incentive for their local managers.

Overall, the aggregate data patterns presented in Tables 3 and 4 suggest differences in both economic behavior across forms and the utilization of organizational forms that are consistent with competition-related moral hazard. However, the differences in Table 2 also suggest systematic selection of different contract types in different environments. This makes it impossible to conclude anything with confidence about the empirical relevance of competition-driven moral hazard at this

Table 4: Variation in Economic Behavior across Market Structure and Contract Forms

Variable	Obs	Mean	Std. Dev.	Obs	Mean	Std. Dev.
		Integrated			*Separated*	
Zero Affiliated						
Regular	236	108.40	15.47	1428	119.31	11.89
Super	236	119.10	13.74	1426	128.53	11.88
Premium	236	128.29	13.01	1428	136.71	11.48
1(Appearance)	308	0.17	0.38	1519	0.12	0.33
Unaffiliated Competitors	308	7.58	6.74	1519	6.98	5.34
One Affiliated						
Regular	170	106.73	17.69	977	118.63	12.21
Super	170	118.05	16.20	976	128.78	12.11
Premium	170	127.16	15.94	977	136.62	11.63
1(Appearance)	217	0.25	0.43	1029	0.12	0.33
Unaffiliated Competitors	217	9.54	6.59	1029	9.65	5.97
Two Affiliated						
Regular	126	106.71	17.91	661	117.97	12.57
Super	126	118.63	16.11	661	128.29	12.11
Premium	126	127.84	15.42	661	136.04	11.62
1(Appearance)	155	0.28	0.45	703	0.15	0.35
Unaffiliated Competitors	155	11.96	7.77	703	11.53	6.79
> Two Affiliated						
Regular	125	103.08	13.95	576	117.08	13.33
Super	125	114.48	12.31	576	126.89	13.07
Premium	125	123.65	11.45	576	134.90	12.14
1(Appearance)	143	0.36	0.48	613	0.12	0.32
Unaffiliated Competitors	143	16.11	8.56	613	13.02	7.27

stage. To obtain a more precise understanding, I therefore move to econometric frameworks that exploit within and between station variation in the data.

5 Strategic Form Choice

5.1 Identification and Inference

In this section, I assess whether gasoline refiners respond to the potential for competition-driven moral hazard by varying their utilization of vertically separated contracts. As noted above in section 2, there also are reasons to believe that there are contracting complementarities that affect the relative desirability of vertically separated forms. Therefore, it is possible that the presence of local affiliates under different contracts have different effects on the desirability of using a vertically separated form at a specific outlet.

I accommodate the possibility of both competition-driven moral hazard and monitoring efficiencies in the following estimating equation of vertically integrated refiners' decision to utilize a vertically separated contract:

$$F_{it} = A_{it}\delta + S_{it}\alpha + N_{it}\rho + X_{it}\lambda + Z_i\nu + u_{it}, \tag{1}$$

where i and t index stations and time of observation, respectively. (For the sake of concision, I suppress market subscripts.) F is a binary variable taking the value of one if station i is vertically separated at time t; A indicates the local market presence of the principal affiliated with station i at that time; S indicates the share of affiliated outlets in the county that are operated under vertically separated contracts; and N is the number of other competitors in the zipcode.[23] X_{it} and Z_i continute to represent time-varying and time invariant station characteristics, respectively, while u_{it} is information unobservable to the econometrician.

The coefficients of interest are δ and α. Respectively, these account for the direct impact of

---

[23]See footnote [20] above for details on the usage of county vs. zipcode level data.

the number of affiliated outlets in the zipcode and the impact of the share of outlets in the county that are contemporaneously organized as separated on the likelihood of using a vertically separated contractual form. By including S as well as A, I am able to separately consider the influence of competition-driven moral hazard and monitoring complementarities on form choice. The stories outlined above in section 2 predicts a negatively signed δ and a positive α.

In terms of the market competition variables, Equation (3) implies linear effects from the different types of competitors, as in Davis (2006). (However, the inclusion of S allows for the possibility of non-linearity from the type of contracts at comparatively proximate stations.) As described further below, I check the importance of the linearity assumptions, and find that the paper's results are qualitatively robust to non-linear alternatives.

In addition to the observable explanatory variables discussed in the previous section, I include brand and state-date indicator variables in all regressions.[24] Thus, I ensure that my estimates are based off of variation within brands, dates, and region, avoiding the possibility of confusing the impact of form with temporally or regulatorily driven differences as well as the possibility of idiosyncratic brand strategies. This is important because Hosken et al. (2008) show that different gasoline chains pursue different pricing strategies, while the existence and severity of divorcement laws varies across the sample regions (Vita, 2000, Blass and Carlton, 2001). Moreover, New Image collected prices at different stations on separate days within a given year; however, the data were collected on the same day within regions.

In estimating Equation (1), the concern is that there will be a systematic connection between market structure and contractual type not being accounted for by the observable information. This is a possibility that must be taken seriously. Unfortunately, with the available data, it is difficult to entirely rule it out; however, I am able to estimate Equation (1) in a variety of different ways. By varying the stringency of the assumptions required for each apprach, I can examine how sensitive the results are to endogeneity concerns.

---

[24]The results are qualitatively similar when I include less parsimonious sets of controls.

In general, I assume that the unobserved information is a composite term, i.e., $u_{it} = \mu_i + \epsilon_{it}$, where μ_i represents time-invariant station-specific heterogeneity and ϵ_{it} is the idiosyncratic error. Depending on μ's correlation with the explanatory variables and the dependent variable, Equation 3 should be estimated in different ways.

First, I make the strong assumption that the station-specific heterogeneity is uncorrelated with the other explanatory variables. This implies that I can estimate equation (3) using ordinary least squares (OLS), accounting for the possible correlations over time at the station-level by clustering or the use of random effects (RE). Insofar as clustering allows for more general correlation structures than RE, it is a more conservative approach.

When the assumption of independence between the unobserved and observed factors does not hold, the cross-sectional estimates suffer from omitted variable bias. Therefore, in my second approach to identification, I include the station-level means of the time-varying regressors to capture the correlation between μ and the observables. This approach stems from Mundlak (1978), who noted that the results from standard linear fixed effects (FE) models can be obtained in a RE model if the means of time-varying regressors are included. Thus, my second approach involves assuming that:

$$\mu_i = \bar{X}_i \xi + v_i, \qquad (2)$$

where $\bar{X}_i$ is the vector of station-level means of time-varying regressors, and v_i represents time invariant station information that is uncorrelated with the observables.

Unfortunately, few elements in my data exhibit much variation over time as station characteristics are largely fixed. For this reason, along with the means of population, income, and number of stations (affiliated and not) in the zipcode, I include the mean lagged volume of sales, and the mean of lagged price of regular unleaded. In addition, I include the one-period lagged terms directly in the Mundlak models. The lagged terms can reasonably be thought to be exogenous (or at least predetermined) at the time the decision-maker chooses forms. While including the lagged terms (and their means) helps control for unobserved heterogeneity, it requires that all stations in MN, OH, and CO are dropped since only one year of data is available for those areas. As with the cross-sectional models, I assume that correlations introduced by the remaining unobservable station-specific heterogeneity can be addressed by clustering the standard errors at the station level. My results are qualitatively robust to the exclusion of the lagged terms.

Third, both of the previous approaches implicitly assume that the refiners can update their contract choices each year. This assumption is quite strong insofar as Blair and Lafontaine (2005) state that franchising contracts are usually many years long. Therefore, I relax the implicit assumption and utilize only the first observation in the data for each station. When taking this approach, I utilize the entire pool of stations in the sample and do not include the Mundlak controls.

Finally, it is worth considering what it would mean if the approaches described above failed to appropriately control for the possible interrelatedness of choices and unobservables. Suppose there were shocks that increased the expected profits from locating multiple stations in a given zipcode. In order to produce systematically biased results, these shocks would have to be correlated with the payoffs to choosing different contracts. To a large extent, therefore, I believe controlling for the share of local outlets organized under vertically separated contracts should capture any systematic correlation.

I estimate all models as probits, allowing for heteroskedastic standard errors, which are clustered at the station-level when there are multiple periods of data per station. Coefficients and standard errors are for numerically calculated marginal effects.

5.2 Empirical Results

Table 5 shows the results of the models of contract choice. Column 1 represents the baseline approach, exploiting observations from all states. Column 2 employs the same estimating approach but replaces the contemporaneous share of nearby outlets that are separated with its one year

Table 5: Market Structure and Form Choice

	All	All, Lag	All, Panel	Initial
	Probit mfx/se	Probit mfx/se	Probit mfx/se	Probit mfx/se
Local Presence	-0.011**	-0.010+	-0.013+	-0.015**
	0	0.01	0.01	0.01
Share Separated	0.197***	0.153**	0.177**	0.287***
	0.04	0.07	0.07	0.06
Competitors	0.001	0.004**	0.001	-0.001
	0	0	0	0
C-Store	0	0.005	0.022	-0.003
	0.01	0.02	0.03	0.02
Service Bays	0.132***	0.106***	0.076***	0.198***
	0.02	0.02	0.02	0.02
Nozzles	-0.004***	-0.003***	0	-0.006***
	0	0	0	0
Population	-0.000*	0	0.001	-0.000***
	0	0	0	0
Income	0	0	0.001	0.001
	0	0	0	0
Brand Effects	Yes	Yes	Yes	Yes
State-Date Effects	Yes	Yes	Yes	Yes
Observations	2725	943	898	1588

* $p<0.10$, ** $p<0.05$, *** $p<0.01$ in two-sided tests. + $p<0.10$ in one-sided test. Estimates are numerically-calculated marginal effects. All standard errors clustered at station-level. Mundlak models include one year lagged volume of sales as well as station-level means of the number of stations in the zipcode, population, and income data.

lag. Column 3 is the Mundlak model, which increases the degree to which time invariant station heterogeneity is controlled for. Column 4 uses only the first observation for each station to control for the possibility that there are frictions impeding the regular updating of form choices.

The results across all four models are similar in the economic and statistical significance of their estimates. Moreover, they are consistent with the theory of competition-driven moral hazard laid out above. In all four models, I find that an increase in the number of affiliated outlets in the vicinity leads to a economically significant lower likelihood of utilizing vertically separated contracts. The impact is not overwhelmingly large as the estimates imply that the presence of one additional affiliated outlet reduces the likelihood of vertical separation by 1.1 to 2 percent. However, insofar as the unconditional likelihood of company-ownership is only 13 percent, the results indicate that the presence of just one affiliated outlet leads to a 10-15 percent increase in the likelihood that the form is utilized.

In addition to supporting the idea that competition can lead to incentive conflicts with vertically separated managers, the Table provides robust evidence in support of the idea that there are scale monitoring efficiencies. This can be seen in the fact that an increase in the share of outlets in the surrounding county operated under a vertically separated form leads to an increase in the likelihood that a specific outlet is also operated at arms length from the principal. Column 2 suggests that this effect is not driven by possible simultaneity of form choices.

The other explanatory variables have coefficients in broad alignment with past research. In general, the presence of other competitors has no economically or statistically significant influence on form choice. There is no influence to having a convenience store on vertical separation. This finding may reflect the influence of aggregating all of the different vertically separated forms as Shepard (1993) found this factor to differentially affect the likelihood of different vertically separated contracts.[25] By contrast, the presence of a service bay significantly increases the likelihood that the refiner uses an arms length arrangement. Broadly consistent with the past literature considering

---

[25] The results of the multinomial logit model presented in Table B-4 support this possibility.

the effect of outlet size on the boundaries of the firm as surveyed in Lafontaine and Slade (2007), I find that the number of nozzles has a negative impact on the likelihood of vertical separation. Finally, I find that neither population nor income is an economically significant factor.

Overall, the results of the form choice models offer strong additional support for the idea that there is competition-driven moral hazard and that it is an empirically significant factor in this industry. The data show that refiners vary their utilization of vertically separated contracts to minimize its likelihood. In addition, as noted above, the key implication regarding the impact of nearby outlets holds when all contract possibilities are endogenized in a multinomial logit setting. Moreover, the results also were robust to the inclusion of controls for the relative presence of inde-pendents and controlling for brand-state-date heterogeneity. Finally, as might have been expected given the discussion of possible endogeneity bias above, the results are robust to instrumenting for the number of affiliated outlets with its one period (station-level) lag.[26] Details on all models not included in the paper are available upon request.

6 Economic Behavior Analysis

6.1 Identification and Inference

The previous section demonstrated that refiners hesitate to employ vertically separated contracts when there are affiliated present in the zipcode. While consistent with concerns about competition-driven moral hazard, one might nevertheless wonder if firms were reacting to other incentives. Alternatively, one might fear that the results were systematically biased as a result of not satisfac-torily addressing the simultaneous determination of form and local market structure. To partially check that this is not leading to inappropriate support for the idea that market structure can produce moral hazard, this section tests for behavioral differences across vertically separated and integrated stations in different market structures conditional on the refiners' choices of contracts.

In order to infer the empirical significance of competition-induced moral hazard on these en-

---

[26]In this regression, however, the monitoring efficiency variable is no longer statistically significant.

dogenous variables, I estimate variations on the following linear general form:

$$Y_{it} = F_{it}\delta + A_{it}\alpha + F \cdot A_{it}\sigma + N_{it}\rho + X_{it}\lambda + Z_i\nu + u_{it}, \tag{3}$$

where i and t again index stations and time of observation, respectively. Y is the economic outcome of interest (i.e., price or quality), and will be the price of regular, super, and premium gasoline or the provision of quality as proxied for by a binary station appearance variable. As before, F indicates whether a given station operates under a vertically separated contract,while A captures the number of affiliated outlets in the market. $F \cdot A$ the interaction between F and A. Once more, N represents the sum of all other gasoline stations in the zipcode; X_{it} are time-varying station and market characteristics; Z_i are time-invariant station characteristics; and u_{it} is information unobservable to the econometrician.

Equation (3) takes a difference in differences approach to trying to identify the impact of moral hazard by high-powered agents on station behavior in multi-product markets. The coefficient of interest is σ, which captures the systematic impact of an additional affiliated station on the behavior of stations operated under vertically separated contracts relative to vertically integrated stations in otherwise similarly structured markets. Any direct impact of vertical separation upon behavior is picked up by δ, while α reveals the direct influence of an additional affiliated outlet on a station's behavior, regardless of whether or not it is operated under a vertically separated contract.

As in Vita (2000) and Hosken et al. (2008), I estimate the pricing models in levels; however, the results are qualitatively identical when I employ a log-linear specification. For the quality of station appearance regressions, I estimate the likelihood of having high quality using probit models, reporting the numerically calculated marginal effects of the explanatory variables. In estimating the pricing models, I exploit only the pooled (with clustering) and Mundlak estimating approaches insofar as there is no reason to fear that gasoline prices are sticky. However, as noted above, there is reason to think that appearance quality is likely to be more durable. Therefore, when exploring the

25

relationship between quality, market structure, and vertical separation, I again estimate a model that uses only the initial observations for each station.

In the price models, I include contemporaneous quality as an explanatory variable. This may strike some as problematic. However, I believe that it is reasonable to treat quality as predetermined at the time prices are chosen. Station quality is likely to be labor intensive and relatively durable; by contrast, prices can be changed rapidly to reflect alterations to supply or demand.

Before turning to the estimation results, I believe it is worth discussing the possibility that the estimating approaches do not fully address the possibility of endogeneity. After all, I largely assume that after conditioning on observables – sometime including the Mundlak variables – that both market structure and contract form can be taken as predetermined. There is no question that this is a very strong assumption. However, I would argue that there is little reason for concern about endogeneity falsely driving results consistent with competition-driven moral hazard. Because of the differences-in-differences approach, this would require shocks positively affecting the desirability of more stations and the usage of vertically separated contracts, but negatively impacting economic behavior. It is difficult to identify such shocks' possible origins in this institutional setting. Indeed, the most intuitive assumption about shocks that impact the number of outlets and vertical separation would relate to demand-side factors. These would be more likely to lead to upward pressure on prices and quality. Thus, I believe that finding a negatively signed σ would represent particularly conservative evidence of the impact of competition-driven moral hazard. As discussed further below, robustness results from instrumental variables exploiting some of the implications of section 5 are consistent with this.

6.2 Empirical Results

6.2.1 Gasoline Prices

Table 6 shows the results of the cross-sectional and Mundlak specifications for regular, super, and premium unleaded gasoline. Columns 1, 3, and 5 show the results of the pooled cross-sectional

Table 6: Form, Market Structure, and Pricing Behavior

	Regular Unleaded		Super Unleaded		Premium Unleaded	
	OLS b/se	Mundlak b/se	OLS b/se	Mundlak b/se	OLS b/se	Mundlak b/se
Separated	0.662*	1.625***	0.625+	2.654***	0.656+	2.423***
	0.34	0.45	0.42	0.63	0.43	0.71
Sep X Local	-0.230*	-0.272*	-0.295*	-0.398*	-0.328**	-0.215
	0.13	0.15	0.15	0.22	0.16	0.25
Local Presence	0.172+	0.102	0.18	0.290+	0.14	0.165
	0.12	0.15	0.14	0.22	0.15	0.25
Competitors	-0.078***	-0.071	-0.051***	0.017	-0.058***	0.048
	0.01	0.07	0.02	0.09	0.02	0.1
C-Store	-0.697***	-0.3	0.042	-0.156	-0.402+	-0.243
	0.21	0.25	0.29	0.31	0.29	0.37
Service Bays	0.677***	0.499**	1.070***	0.571*	1.173***	0.727**
	0.2	0.25	0.27	0.32	0.26	0.34
Appearance	-0.295*	-0.864***	0.258	-0.892**	-0.107	-0.796*
	0.18	0.3	0.22	0.41	0.25	0.48
Population	0	-0.011	0	-0.041	0	0.034
	0	0.03	0	0.03	0	0.04
Income	0.098***	0.025	0.138***	0.185*	0.156***	0.061
	0.01	0.09	0.01	0.1	0.01	0.11
Brand Effects	Yes	Yes	Yes	Yes	Yes	Yes
State-Date Effects	Yes	Yes	Yes	Yes	Yes	Yes
Observations	4299	1616	4296	1616	4299	1616

* $p<0.10$, ** $p<0.05$, *** $p<0.01$ in two-sided tests. + $p<0.10$ in one-sided test. All standard errors clustered at station-level. Mundlak models include one year lagged volume of sales as well as station-level means of lagged volumes, the number of stations in the zipcode, population, and income data.

models. Columns 2, 4, and 6 show the results of the Mundlak models when I more extensively control for unobserved heterogeneity.

The results of the different models are consistent with the theory outlined above. In all six regressions, the interaction term's coefficient is negative. Moreover, in five of the models, the coefficient is statistically significant at conventional levels. The negative coefficients indicate that as the number of nearby affiliated stations increases, vertically separated stations cut their prices more than vertically integrated outlets. Although the magnitude of the coefficient on the interaction effect appears small – between 0.2 and 0.4 cents per affiliated station – these effects are of non-trivial economic significance because retail margins in gasoline retailing are very low. Hosken et al. (2008) and Kleit (2005) report that retail margins average 20 cents or less. Thus, a one standard deviation in the number of affiliated stations in a zipcode leads to a price change equal to 1-3 percent or more of the average retail margin. Furthermore, it is worth noting that these results represent conservative estimates of the impact of competition-driven moral hazard insofar as they represent the net effect of price cutting induced by moral hazard and price-increasing promotional externalities and/or monitoring effects.

The estimated coefficients for the market structure and vertical contracting variables are also in line with the past literature. As in Wilson (2011b), I always find that the vertically separated stations charge higher prices and that these effects are significantly larger and more precisely estimated when I control for unobserved station-level factors. Consistent with the idea that affiliated stations are likely to be particularly close substitutes for consumers, making their diversion ratios especially large, I find that the presence of affiliated stations in and of itself exerts upward pressure on station pricing. The effect of this term is never statistically significant at conventional levels in two-sided tests, however. Finally, I intuitively find that the presence of unaffiliated competitors generally exerts downward pressure on station pricing.

The effects of the other control variables also are all consistent with theory and previous empirical work. The theoretical models presented in Slade (1996) and Wilson (2011b) predict that stations offering products that complement gasoline sales should have lower gasoline prices. This is consistent with the finding that the presence of a convenience store is negatively correlated with gasoline price. I also find that service capabilities are associated with higher prices, which is consistent with the findings of Slade (1996). Interestingly, I find that stations with higher quality appearances tend to have lower prices, which may suggest cost complementarities between the provision of quality and other desired services. Finally, the results show higher household incomes are associated with higher prices; however, population's impact is negligible and inconsistently signed.

Overall, these results offer significant support for the importance of competition-driven moral hazard. They are consistent with the idea that vertically separated stations engage in tougher price competition in the presence of affiliated outlets than would vertically integrated stations in otherwise equivalent situations. Such behavior is in line with the idea that the high-powered local managers at vertically separated outlets do not internalize the impact of their competitive decisions on overall brand performance. As noted above, the results represent particularly conservative estimates insofar as they represent net effects, and there may be some demand advantages to using vertically separated contracts in markets with affiliated outlets.

Furthermore, although not shown here, the price results are robust to a host of alternative specifications including controling for the relative presence of independent stations, adding brand-specific state-year dummies to reduce concern that the results are driven by brand-specific variation across geographic areas, and using non-linear logarithmic formulations of the market structure variables as in Berry (1992). Moreover, the price regression results are qualitatively robust to instrumenting for the choice of vertical contract and the interaction term with the share of affiliates in the county that are operated under vertically separated forms, the number of gasoline nozzles at the station, and the one year lag of affiliated stations in the zipcode. However, it must be noted that while instrumenting leads to coefficients of the same signs but significantly larger magnitudes (as in Wilson (2011b)) as the OLS and Mundlak models, the results are not precisely identified. This is not surprising given the high degree of correlation between the endogenous variables and the dramatic reduction in the sample size that instrumenting with lags leads to. Consistent with such problems, F tests of the explanatory power of the instruments in the first stage are somewhat marginal, and C tests of the exogeneity of the instruments cannot reject their endogeneity. Because of these things, I do not place great weight on the IV point estimates and do not report them here.

6.2.2 Quality of Station Appearance

Table 7 shows the results of models of the determinants of high quality station appearances. Column 1 uses observations from all states, while Column 2 represents the discrete choice analogue to the linear Mundlak models estimated for prices. Finally, Column 3 uses only the first observation for each station to control for the possibility that appearance is "sticky" in some way. If this were the case, it would be inappropriate to treat multiple observations for a station as equivalent.

As with the price models, the estimation results are generally consistent with the theory outlined above, and are qualitatively similar across models and data samples. In all three models, the interaction term is negative as predicted. However, the term is only statistically significant in the first and third models. Moreover, the economic magnitude of the coefficient on the interaction term is also markedly larger in these models. Indeed, for almost all of the explanatory variables, the Mundlak model recovers coefficients that are statistically and economically less significant than in the other models. These findings may reflect the comparative stickiness of the appearance variable, particularly given the very short panel. Hence, appearance is likely to be correlated with the time invariant station-level heterogeneity that is partially controlled for with lags and time-varying means in the Mundlak model. Therefore, I place greater emphasis on the estimates from Columns 1 and 3, which imply that each additional affiliated outlet in a local market reduces the likelihood that a vertically separated station has a high quality appearance by 2 or 3 percent. While not enormous, such effects represent a shift of 16-20 percent relative to the unconditional likelihood that a vertically separated outlet has a high quality appearance.

In addition, I find results generally in line with the prior literature for the other form and

Table 7: Form, Market Structure, and Product Quality

	Full	Mundlak	Initial
	Probit mfx/se	Probit mfx/se	Probit mfx/se
Separated	-0.114***	-0.026	-0.137***
	0.03	0.03	0.04
Sep X Local	-0.018**	-0.008	-0.032***
	0.01	0.01	0.01
Local Presence	0.002	-0.007	0.006
	0.01	0.01	0.01
Competitors	0.002**	-0.005	0.002*
	0	0	0
C-Store	-0.011	0.02	-0.029+
	0.02	0.02	0.02
Service Bays	-0.181***	-0.129***	-0.183***
	0.01	0.02	0.02
Population	0.000**	0.001	0.000*
	0	0	0
Income	0.001	-0.004	-0.001
	0	0.01	0
Brand Effects	Yes	Yes	Yes
State-Date Effects	Yes	Yes	Yes
Observations	4015	1247	2474

* $p<0.10$, ** $p<0.05$, *** $p<0.01$ in two-sided tests. + $p<0.10$ in one-sided test. Estimates are the marginal effects. All standard errors clustered at station-level. Mundlak models include one year lagged volume of sales and one year lag of the price of regular unleaded as well as station-level means of lagged volumes, lagged prices, the number of stations in the zipcode, population, and income data.

market structure variables. Vertical separation is associated with lower likelihood of a high quality appearance, which is consistent with the simple comparisons of means shown above. In addition, the presence of competitors appears to put upward pressure on the provision of quality though this effect is of small magnitude. This result is supportive of the idea that stations attract customers in part by offering them a more pleasing experience than competitors. By contrast, there is no economically or statistically significant separate effect for the additional presence of affiliated outlets.

The coefficients on the other controls also are broadly intuitive. The presence of both convenience stores and service bays reduces the likelihood that a station has a high quality appearance. This is consistent with the necessity of allocating finite effort across a variety of tasks. If revenues are generated from two separate activities for which demand is inversely correlated, then the incentive to devote resources to an activity that only benefits one of them is reduced, especially if it is lower margin. This may explain why service bays have a larger and more statistically significant effect (Slade, 1996). Population and income have economically insignificant impacts.

Overall, the findings for the connection between local market structure, vertical separation, and the provision of quality offer significant additional support for the empirical relevance of competition-driven moral hazard. As before, these results were robust to controlling for the relative presence of independent competitors and the possibility of brand-state-date heterogeneity. In addition, as noted above in footnote [15], robustness checks exploiting the full range of quality grades returned qualitatively similar results when estimated as ordered probit models.

7 Conclusion

This article advances the idea that market structure differentially influences the strategic incentives of outlets operated under different types of vertical contracts. As a result, market structure should also influence the choice of contractual form. Investigating the empirical importance of these factors in the context of the retail gasoline industry, I find that gasoline stations operated under vertically separated contracts charge lower prices, while neglecting to maintain high quality appearances, when they are in the presence of affiliated stations than do vertically integrated stations. Consistent with this, I show that the refiners are more likely to employ vertically separated contracts in areas where such moral hazard problems are less likely to arise. All of these findings support the idea that vertical separation can lead to incentive conflicts between agent and principal in multi-product markets.

Overall, the paper shows how factors like market structure and a menu of products, which industrial economists are increasingly focusing on in other areas, can be incorporated into principal-agent settings. In addition, my results are relevant to practitioners and policy-makers interested in retail gasoline markets. This is because several vertically integrated refiners (e.g., Exxon) have indicated a desire to stop having company-owned and operated stations (MSNBC, 2008). This paper suggests that their decisions will have an influence on product market conditions. In particular, ceteris paribus, it suggests that, at least in the short run, prices will fall, but so too will station quality, making overall welfare effects ambiguous. I hope to investigate these issues further in subsequent research.

References

Barron, J.M. and J.R. Umbeck, "Effects of Different Contractual Arrangements: The Case of Retail Gasoline Markets," *Journal of Law & Economics*, 1984, *27*, 313–328.

Berry, S., "Estimation of a Model of Entry in the Airline Industry," *Econometrica*, 1992, pp. 889–917.

— **and J. Waldfogel**, "Product Quality and Market Size," *The Journal of Industrial Economics*, 2010, *58* (1).

Blair, R.D. and F. Lafontaine, *The Economics of Franchising*, Cambridge University Press, 2005.

— **and** — , "Understanding the Economics of Franchising and the Laws That Regulate It," *Franchise Law Journal*, 2006, *26*, 55.

Blass, A.A. and D.W. Carlton, "Choice of Organization Form in Gasoline Retailing and the Cost of Laws That Limit That Choice," *Journal of Law & Economics*, 2001, *44*, 511–524.

Brickley, J.A., "Incentive Conflicts and Contractual Restraints: Evidence from Franchising," *Journal of Law & Economics*, 1999, *42* (2), 745–74.

— **and F.H. Dark**, "The choice of organizational form: The case of franchising," *Journal of Financial Economics*, 1987, *18* (2), 401–420.

— , — , **and M.S. Weisbach**, "Economic Effects of Franchise Termination Laws, The," *Journal of Law & Economics*, 1991, *34*, 101.

Bronnenberg, Bart, Jean-Pierre Dube, and M. Gentzkow, "The Evolution of Brand Preferences: Evidence from Consumer Migration," *University of Chicago, mimeo*, 2010.

— , **Sanjay K. Dhar, and Jean-Pierre Dube**, "Brand History, Geography, and the Persistence of Brand Shares," *Journal of Political Economy*, 2009, *117* (1), 87 – 115.

Davis, P.J., "Measuring the Business Stealing, Cannibalization and Market Expansion Effects of Entry in the US Motion Picture Exhibition Market," *Journal of Industrial Economics*, 2006, *54* (3), 293–321.

DeBonis, M., "D.C. attorney general investigating gas station owner," *Washington Post*, 2011.

Ellickson, P., "Supermarkets as a Natural Oligopoly?," *Economic Inquiry*, forthcoming.

Forbes, S.J. and M. Lederman, "Does vertical integration affect firm performance? Evidence from the airline industry," *The RAND Journal of Economics*, 2010, *41* (4), 765–790.

Grossman, S.J. and O.D. Hart, "The costs and benefits of ownership: A theory of vertical and lateral integration," *The Journal of Political Economy*, 1986, *94* (4), 691–719.

Hadfield, Gillian K., "Credible Spatial Preemption through Franchising," *The RAND Journal of Economics*, 1991, *22* (4), pp. 531–543.

Hart, O. and J. Moore, "Property Rights and the Nature of the Firm," *Journal of Political Economy*, 1990, *98* (6), 1119–1158.

Holmstrom, B. and P. Milgrom, "Multitask principal-agent analyses: Incentive contracts, asset ownership, and job design," *Journal of Law, Economics, & Organization*, 1991, *7* (special issue), 24–52.

Hosken, D.S., R.S. McMillan, and C.T. Taylor, "Retail gasoline pricing: What do we know?," *International Journal of Industrial Organization*, 2008, *26* (6), 1425–1436.

Jin, G.Z. and P. Leslie, "Reputational incentives for restaurant hygiene," *American Economic Journal: Microeconomics*, 2009, *1* (1), 237–267.

Kalnins, A., "An empirical analysis of territorial encroachment within franchised and company-owned branded chains," *Marketing Science*, 2004, pp. 476–489.

— **and F. Lafontaine**, "Multi-unit ownership in franchising: evidence from the fast-food industry in Texas," *RAND Journal of Economics*, 2004, pp. 747–761.

Klein, B., "Transaction cost determinants of "unfair" contractual arrangements," *The American Economic Review*, 1980, *70* (2), 356–362.

— , "The economics of franchise contracts," *Journal of Corporate Finance*, 1995, *2* (1-2), 9–37.

Kleit, A.N., "The Economics of Gasoline Retailing: Petroleum Distribution and Retailing Issues in the U. S," *Energy Studies Review*, 2005, *13* (2), 1–28.

Kosova, R., F. Lafontaine, and R. Perrigot, "Organizational Form and Performance: Evidence from the Hotel Industry," *Cornell University, mimeo*, 2010.

Krueger, A.B., "Ownership, Agency, and Wages: An Examination of Franchising in the Fast Food Industry," *The Quarterly Journal of Economics*, 1991, *106* (1), 75.

Laffont, J.J. and D. Martimort, *The Theory of Incentives: The Principal-Agent Model*, Princeton University Press, 2002.

Lafontaine, F. and M. Slade, "Vertical integration and firm boundaries: the evidence," *Journal of Economic Literature*, 2007, *45* (3), 629–685.

__ , **R. Perrigot, and N.E. Wilson**, "Institutional Quality and Organizational Form Decisions: Evidence from Within the Firm," *working paper*, 2011.

Mazzeo, M.J., "Product choice and oligopoly market structure," *The RAND Journal of Economics*, 2002, pp. 221–242.

Meyer, D. and J. Fischer, "The Economics of Price Zones and Territorial Restrictions in Gasoline Marketing," *Federal Trade Commission Bureau of Economics Working Paper*, 2004, *271*.

Michael, S.C., "The effect of organizational form on quality: the case of franchising," *Journal of Economic Behavior & Organization*, 2000, *43* (3), 295–318.

MSNBC, "Exxon to sell all of companys gas stations," *MSNBC.com*, 2008.

Mundlak, Y., "On the pooling of time series and cross section data," *Econometrica*, 1978, pp. 69–85.

Novak, S. and S. Stern, "How does outsourcing affect performance dynamics? Evidence from the automobile industry," *Management Science*, 2008, *54* (12), 1963–1979.

Shepard, A., "Contractual form, retail price, and asset characteristics in gasoline retailing," *RAND Journal of Economics*, 1993, *24* (1), 58–77.

Slade, M.E., "Multitask agency and contract choice: an empirical exploration," *International Economic Review*, 1996, *37* (2), 465–486.

Sutton, J., "Market structure: theory and evidence," *Handbook of Industrial Organization*, 2007, *3*, 2301–2368.

Thomadsen, R., "The effect of ownership structure on prices in geographically differentiated industries," *The RAND Journal of Economics*, 2005, *36* (4), 908–929.

Vita, M.G., "Regulatory restrictions on vertical integration and control: The competitive impact of gasoline divorcement policies," *Journal of Regulatory Economics*, 2000, *18* (3), 217–233.

Williamson, O.E., *Markets and hierarchies, analysis and antitrust implications: a study in the economics of internal organization*, Free Press New York, 1975.

Wilson, N.E., "Branding, Cannibalization, and Spatial Preemption: An Application to the Hotel Industry," *FTC Bureau of Economics, working paper*, 2011.

__ , "The Impact of Vertical Contracting on Firm Behavior: Evidence from Gasoline Stations," *FTC Bureau of Economics, working paper*, 2011.

Winter, R. A., "Antitrust restrictions on single-firm strategies," *Canadian Journal of Economics*, 2009, *42* (4), 1207–1239.

Zhu, T., V. Singh, and M.D. Manuszak, "Market structure and competition in the retail discount industry," *Journal of Marketing Research*, 2009, *46* (4), 453–466.

Appendix A: New Image Data Description

Below, I provide the name and description provided by New Image of those variables used in the analysis and the method by which they were transformed (if appropriate).

- Organizational Form: Categorical variable corresponding to the answer to the following question. TYPE OF OPERATION)(TOO) - Overall status of operation, ask respondent to identify:

  0) - No building or doesn't sell gasoline

  1) - Lessee dealer building and facility owned by major/non major oil company, business owned by dealer. [I reordered this as Type 2.]

  2) - Salary operation building and facility owned by major/non major oil company. Personnel paid by company. [I reordered this as Type 1, so that salaried operations represented the baseline.]

  3) - Open Dealer - Land and operation owned by individual who is supplied product by major/non major oil company.

  4) - Jobber/Wholesaler Operation owned by a local company that owns several operations in the area. (EXP distributor) or a franchise/chain organization (EXP a convenience store chain)

- Regular Unleaded Price: Numerical variable corresponding to non-constrained answer to the following question. OCT REGULAR UNLEADED)(UO) - Price Reg Unleaded)(RUP)

- Super Unleaded Price: Numerical variable corresponding to non-constrained answer to the following question. OCT MIDGRADE UNLEADED)(MO) - Price mid Unleaded)(MUP)

- Premium Unleaded Price: Numerical variable corresponding to non-constrained answer to the following question. OCT SUPER)(SO) - Price Super Unleaded)(PUP)

- Volume: Numerical variable corresponding to non-constrained answer to the following question. MONTHLY VOLUME)(GV) - Enter average number of gallons sold in one month. (last completed month)

- C-Store: Dummy variable which takes value of 1 if an answer other than 0 chosen for the following question. INTERIOR C-STORE APPEARANCE)(INAP) As it appears to consumer.

  0) - No snack shop

  1) - Outstanding (top 10 percent)

  2) - Excellent

  3) - Better than average

  4) - Equal to average

  5) - Below average

  6) - Poor

  7) - Unacceptable (bottom 10 percent)

- Service Bays: Dummy variable which takes value of 1 if a number other than 0 chosen for the following question. SERVICE BAYS)(NOSB) - Total number of service bays. If not in operation mention in comments.

- Appearance: Dummy variable which takes value of 1 if the answer to the following question takes the value of 1 or 2. APPEARANCE OF BUILDING)(AOB) -

  0) - N/A

  1) - Outstanding (top 10 percent)

  2) - Excellent

  3) - Better than average

  4) - Equal to average

  5) - Below average

  6) - poor

  7) - Unacceptable (bottom 10percent)

- Nozzles: Numerical variable corresponding to non-constrained answer to the following question. GASOLINE NOZZLES)(GN) - Total number of gasoline only nozzles. Do not include diesel or kerosene.

Appendix B: Additional Tables

Table B-1: Contract Variation Across States

	1996	1997	1998	1999	2000	Total
CO	0	0	0	630	0	630
	0	*0*	*0*	*100*	*0*	*100*
DC	0	117	0	109	0	226
	0	*51.77*	*0*	*48.23*	*0*	*100*
KY	239	237	0	244	0	720
	33.19	*32.92*	*0*	*33.89*	*0*	*100*
MD	0	437	0	444	0	881
	0	*49.6*	*0*	*50.4*	*0*	*100*
MN	0	0	0	600	0	600
	0	*0*	*0*	*100*	*0*	*100*
OH	0	0	0	0	185	185
	0	*0*	*0*	*0*	*100*	*100*
VA	0	478	482	485	0	1,445
	0	*33.08*	*33.36*	*33.56*	*0*	*100*
Total	239	1,269	482	2,512	185	4,687
	5.1	*27.07*	*10.28*	*53.6*	*3.95*	*100*

Rows in *italics* represent percentages.

Table B-2: Station-Period Observations by State and Form

State	Company Owned	Lessee Dealer	Open Dealer	Jobber	Total
CO	290	57	99	184	630
	46.03	*9.05*	*15.71*	*29.21*	*100*
DC	0	154	43	2	199
	0	*77.39*	*21.61*	*1.01*	*100*
KY	49	74	233	364	720
	6.81	*10.28*	*32.36*	*50.56*	*100*
MD	14	619	157	44	834
	1.68	*74.22*	*18.82*	*5.28*	*100*
MN	57	95	198	250	600
	9.5	*15.83*	*33*	*41.67*	*100*
OH	70	15	45	55	185
	37.84	*8.11*	*24.32*	*29.73*	*100*
VA	191	749	307	120	1,367
	13.97	*54.79*	*22.46*	*8.78*	*100*
Total	671	1,763	1,082	1,019	4,535
	14.8	*38.88*	*23.86*	*22.47*	*100*

Rows in *italics* represent percentages.

Table B-3: Multiple Contract Behavioral Regressions

	Regular Unleaded		Quality	
	OLS b/se	Mundlak b/se	Probit mfx/se	Mundlak mfx/se
Lessee	0.861**	1.454***	-0.075***	-0.024
	0.35	0.42	0.02	0.03
Lessee X Local	-0.238*	-0.229+	-0.020**	-0.008
	0.14	0.16	0.01	0.01
Open	0.901**	1.554***	-0.116***	0.019
	0.43	0.52	0.02	0.04
Open X Local	-0.1	-0.347*	-0.011	-0.018
	0.19	0.2	0.01	0.02
Jobber	0.033	0.948+	-0.074***	-0.042*
	0.4	0.64	0.02	0.02
Jobber X Local	-0.214+	-0.177	-0.021**	0.007
	0.16	0.2	0.01	0.02
Local Presence	0.154	0.078	0.002	-0.006
	0.12	0.15	0.01	0.01
Competitors	-0.080***	-0.066	0.002**	-0.006+
	0.01	0.07	0	0
Nozzles			0.001+	-0.003***
			0	0
C-Store	-0.634***	-0.342+	-0.019	0.021+
	0.2	0.25	0.02	0.01
Service Bays	0.429**	0.405+	-0.175***	-0.132***
	0.21	0.27	0.01	0.02
Population	0	-0.02	0.000*	0.001
	0	0.03	0	0
Income	0.099***	0.028	0.001	-0.005
	0.01	0.09	0	0.01
Brand Effects	Yes	Yes	Yes	Yes
State-Date Effects	Yes	Yes	Yes	Yes
Observations	4298	1615	4015	1247

* $p<0.10$, ** $p<0.05$, *** $p<0.01$ in two-sided tests. + $p<0.10$ in one-sided test. Probit estimates are numerically calculated marginal effects. All standard errors clustered at station-level. Mundlak price model contains lagged volume and mean number of outlets, lagged volume, income, and population. Mundlak quality model contains lagged volume and price as well as mean number of outlets, lagged volume, lagged price, income, and population.

Table B-4: Multinomial Logit Model of Contract Choice

	Lessee b/se	Open b/se	Jobber b/se
Local Presence	-0.114	-0.161+	-0.122
	0.09	0.1	0.11
Share Separated	1.743**	2.580***	4.661***
	0.77	0.76	0.84
Competitors	0.032*	0.01	0.007
	0.02	0.02	0.02
C-Store	0.089	-0.650**	0.217
	0.23	0.26	0.32
Service Bays	1.977***	2.518***	0.3
	0.27	0.29	0.32
Nozzles	-0.021+	-0.125***	-0.063***
	0.01	0.02	0.01
Population	0	-0.001**	-0.002***
	0	0	0
Income	-0.004	-0.009	0.01
	0.01	0.01	0.01
Brand Effects		Yes	
State Effects		Yes	
Year Effects		Yes	
Observations		3113	

* $p<0.10$, ** $p<0.05$, *** $p<0.01$ in two-sided tests. + $p<0.10$ in one-sided test. Regression utilizes all observations from all states; convergence problems occurred when state-date effects were employed. Standard errors clustered at station-level.

www.ingramcontent.com/pod-product-compliance
Lightning Source LLC
Chambersburg PA
CBHW081240170526
45165CB00009B/3129